I Wander'd
Lonely as a Cloud

Cockermouth

Derwent R.

Keswick

Derwent Water

Buttermere

Ullswater

Thirlmere

Grasmere · *Grasmere*

Blea Tarn

· Ambleside

Hawkshead ·

Coniston ·

Coniston Water

Esthwaite Water

· Windermere

Windermere

Kendal

Irish Sea

Barrow-
in-Furness

THE LAKE DISTRICT

I Wander'd Lonely as a Cloud

✎ THE LAKE POETS ✎

Edited by

ROBIN LANGLEY SOMMER

FOR MAUREEN AND KEITH

Published by Grange Books
An Imprint of Grange Books PLC
Units 1–6, Industrial Estate
Hoo, near Rochester
Kent 3ME 9ND

This edition published 1999

Copyright © 1999 DoveTail Books
Design © Ziga Design
Front cover photograph: Tarn Hows, Cumbria,
© Woodmansterne

Produced in association with Saraband Inc.

ISBN: 1-84013-243-4

Printed in China

9 8 7 6 5 4 3 2 1

Contents

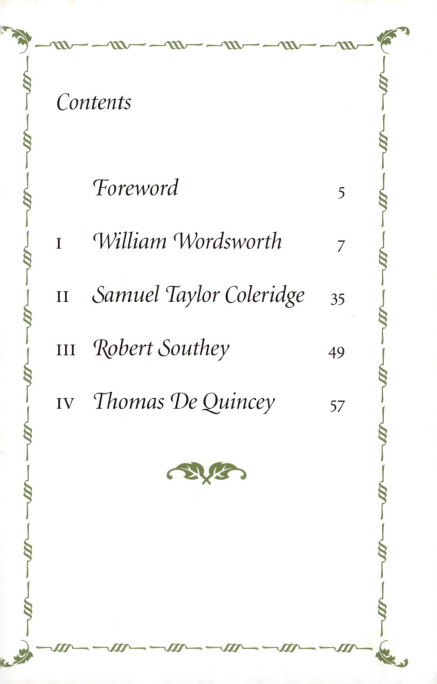

Foreword

The English Romantic movement in poetry began with the publication of the *Lyrical Ballads* (1798) by William Wordsworth and Samuel Taylor Coleridge. Wordsworth had grown up in the beautiful Lake District, and his poetry celebrated the idyllic beauty of his boyhood and youth there. Born at Cockermouth, Cumbria (then Cumberland), he spent most of his life among the lakes and mountains, apart from his years at Cambridge and several trips to Europe. He broke with the classical tradition by writing of nature, everyday people and his own feelings in a simple, natural style.

Wordsworth and the visionary young Coleridge became friends in the Lake District shortly after Coleridge had met Robert Southey, another idealistic young poet who wrote long romantic tales in verse and planned to found a Utopian community; Thomas De Quincey was soon to join the group. The term "Lake Poets" was coined by the *Edinburgh Review* as a derisive commentary on their work, in which passionate imagination and broad spacious verse supplanted the contrived couplets of neoclassicism.

I

William Wordsworth

William Wordsworth
(1770–1850)

*T*he greatest of English Romantic poets came to critical attention in 1798, at the age of twenty-eight, with the publication of the *Lyrical Ballads* with Samuel Taylor Coleridge. It contained his "Lines Composed Above Tintern Abbey," written with such simplicity and clarity that it was widely criticized at the time as unpoetic. Committed to his ideal of a new kind of poetry, Wordsworth continued to write his near-mystical celebrations of nature in such masterpieces as "Ode on Intimations of Immortality" and the long autobiographical poem *The Prelude*, published in 1839 after years of labour. By that time, his genius had been recognised. He was named poet laureate in 1843.

FROM *The Prelude*, BOOK 1

Oh! many a time have I, a five years' child,
A naked boy, in one delightful rill,
A little mill-race severed from his stream,
Made one long bathing of a summer's day,
Basked in the sun, and plunged, and basked again
Alternate all a summer's day, or coursed
Over the sandy field, leaping through groves,
Of yellow grunsel, or when crag and hill,
The woods, and distant Skiddaw's lofty height,
Were bronzed with a deep radiance, stood alone
Beneath the sky, as if I had been born
On Indian Plains, and from my Mother's hut
Had run abroad in wantonness, to sport,
A naked savage, in the thunder shower.

COCKERMOUTH

FROM *The Prelude*, BOOK 1

*A*nd in the frosty season, when the sun
Was set, and visible for many a mile
The cottage windows blazed through twilight
   gloom,
I heeded not their summons: happy time
It was indeed for all of us—for me
It was a time of rapture! Clear and loud
The village clock tolled six,—I wheeled about,
Proud and exulting like an untired horse
That cares not for his home. All shod with steel,
We hissed along the polished ice in games...
So through the darkness and the cold we flew,
And not a voice was idle; with the din
Smitten, the precipices rang aloud;
The leafless trees and every icy crag
Tinkled like iron; while far distant hills
Into the tumult sent an alien sound
Of melancholy not unnoticed, while the stars
Eastward were sparkling clear, and in the west
The orange sky of evening died away.
Not seldom from the uproar I retired
Into a silent bay, or sportively
Glanced sideways, leaving the tumultuous throng,
To cut across the reflex of a star

That fled, and, flying, still before me, gleamed
Upon the glassy plain; and oftentimes,
when we had given our bodies to the wind,
And all the shadowy banks on either side
Came sweeping through the darkness, spinning
   still
The rapid line of motion, then at once
Have I, reclining back upon my heels,
Stopped short; yet still the solitary cliffs
Wheeled by me—even as if the earth had rolled
With visible motion her diurnal round!
Behind me did they stretch in solemn train,
Feebler and feebler, and I stood and watched
Till all was tranquil as a dreamless sleep.

ESTHWAITE

Ode on Intimations of Immortality

*FROM RECOLLECTIONS
OF EARLY CHILDHOOD*

*T*here was a time when meadow, grove, and stream,
The earth, and every common sight
    To me did seem
  Apparell'd in celestial light,
The glory and the freshness of a dream.
It is not now as it has been of yore;—
  Turn wheresoe'er I may,
    By night or day,
The things which I have seen I now can see no
  more!
  The rainbow comes and goes,
  And lovely is the rose;
  The moon doth with delight
Look round her when the heavens are bare;
  Waters on a starry night
  Are beautiful and fair;
The sunshine is a glorious birth;
But yet I know, where'er I go,
That there hath pass'd away a glory from the earth.
Now, while the birds thus sing a joyous song,
And while the young lambs bound

    As to the tabor's sound,
To me alone there came a thought of grief:
A timely utterance gave that thought relief,
    And I again am strong.
The cataracts blow their trumpets from the
    steep,—
No more shall grief of mine the season wrong:
I hear the echoes through the mountains throng,
The winds come to me from the fields of sleep,
    And all the earth is gay;
      Land and sea
Give themselves up to jollity,
    And with the heart of May
Doth every beast keep holiday;—
      Thou Child of Joy
Shout round me, let me hear thy shouts,
Thou happy Shepherd-boy!
Ye blesséd creatures, I have heard the call
    Ye to each other make; I see
The heavens laugh with you in your jubilee;
    My heart is at your festival,
    My head hath its coronal,
The fulness of your bliss, I feel—I feel it all.

O evil day! if I were sullen
    While earth herself is adorning
        This sweet May morning;
    And the children are culling
        On every side,
    In a thousand valleys far and wide,
    Fresh flowers; while the sun shines warm,
And the babe leaps up on his mother's arm:—
    I hear, I hear, with joy I hear!
    —But there's a tree, of many, one,
A single field which I have look'd upon,
Both of them speak of something that is gone:
        The pansy at my feet
        Doth the same tale repeat:
Whither is fled the visionary gleam?
Where is it now, the glory and the dream?

Our birth is but a sleep and a forgetting;
The Soul that rises with us, our life's Star,
    Hath had elsewhere its setting
        And cometh from afar;
    Not in entire forgetfulness,
    And not in utter nakedness,
But trailing clouds of glory do we come
        From God, who is our home:
Heaven lies about us in our infancy!

Shades of the prison-house begin to close
    Upon the growing boy,
But he beholds the light, and whence it flows,
    He sees it in his joy;
The youth, who daily farther from the east
   Must travel, still is Nature's priest,
    And by the vision splendid
    Is on his way attended;
At length the man perceives it die away,
And fade into the light of common day.

My Heart Leaps Up

*M*y heart leaps up when I behold
  A rainbow in the sky:
So was it when my life began,
So is it now I am a man,
So be it when I shall grow old
  Or let me die!
The Child is father of the Man:
And I could wish my days to be
Bound each to each by natural piety.

FROM *The Prelude*, BOOK 5

*T*here was a Boy: ye knew him well, ye cliffs
And islands of Winander!—many a time
At evening, when the earliest stars began
To move along the edges of the hills,
Rising or setting, would he stand alone
Beneath the trees or by the glittering lake.
And there, with fingers interwoven, both hands
Pressed closely palm to palm, and to his mouth
Uplifted, he, as through an instrument,
Blew mimic hootings to the silent owls,
That they might answer him; and they would
    shout
Across the watery vale, and shout again,
Responsive to his call, with quivering peals,
And long halloos and screams, and echoes loud,
Redoubled and redoubled, concourse wild
Of jocund din; and, when a lengthened pause
Of silence came and baffled his best skill,
Then sometimes, in that silence while he hung
Listening, a gentle shock of mild surprise
Has carried far into his heart the voice
Of mountain torrents; or the visible scene
Would enter unawares into his mind,
With all its solemn imagery, its rocks,

Its woods, and that uncertain heaven, received
Into the bosom of the steady lake.

WINDERMERE

FROM *The Excursion*

*W*e scaled, without a track to ease our steps,
A steep ascent; and reached a dreary plain,
With a tumultuous waste of huge hill tops
Before us; savage region! which I paced
Dispirited: when, all at once, behold!
Beneath our feet, a little lowly vale,
A lowly vale, and yet uplifted high
Among the mountains; even as if the spot
Had been from eldest time by wish of theirs
So placed, to be shut out from all the world!
Urn-like it was in shape, deep as an urn;
With rocks encompassed, save that to the south
Was one small opening, where a heath-clad ridge
Supplied a boundary less abrupt and close;
A quiet treeless nook, with two green fields,
A liquid pool that glittered in the sun,
And one bare dwelling; one abode, no more!

BLEA TARN

FROM *Fidelity*

A barking sound the Shepherd hears,
A cry as of a dog or fox;
He halts—and searches with his eyes
Among the scattered rocks:
And now at distance can discern
A stirring in a brake of fern;
And instantly a dog is seen.
Glancing through that covert green.

The Dog is not of mountain breed;
Its motions, too, are wild and shy;
With something, as the Shepherd thinks,
Unusual in its cry:
Nor is there anyone in sight
All round in hollow or on height;
Nor shout, nor whistle strikes his ear;
What is the creature doing here?

It was a cove, a huge recess,
That keeps, till June, December's snow;
A lofty precipice in front,
A silent tarn below!
Far in the bosom of Helvellyn,

Remote from public road or dwelling,
Pathway, or cultivated land;
From trace of human foot or hand.

There sometimes doth a leaping fish
Send through the tarn a lonely cheer;
The crags repeat the raven's croak,
In symphony austere;
Thither the rainbow comes—the cloud —
And mists that spread the flying shroud;
And sunbeams; and the sounding blast,
That, if it could, would hurry past;
But that enormous barrier holds it fast.

RED TARN, HELVELLYN

The Idle Shepherd-Boys;
OR, *Dungeon-Ghyll Force*
A Pastoral

 T he valley rings with mirth and joy;
Among the hills the echoes play
A never never ending song,
To welcome in the May.
The magpie chatters with delight;
The mountain raven's youngling brood
Have left the mother and the nest;
And they go rambling east and west
In search of their own food;
Or through the glittering vapours dart
In very wantonness of heart.

Beaneath a rock, upon the grass,
Two boys are sitting in the sun;
Their work, if any work they have,
Is out of mind—or done.
On pipes of sycamore they play
The fragments of a Christmas hymn;
Or with that plant which in our dale
We call stag-horn, or fox's tail,
Their rusty hats they trim:

And thus, as happy as the day,
Those Shepherds wear the time away.

Along the river's stony marge
The sand-lark chants a joyous song;
The thrush is busy in the wood,
And carols loud and strong.
A thousand lambs are on the rocks,
All newly born! both earth and sky
Keep jubilee, and more than all,
Those boys with their green coronal;
They never hear the cry,
That plantive cry! which up the hill
Comes from the depth of Dungeon-Ghyll.

…

'Cross, if you dare, where I shall cross—
Come on, and tread where I shall tread.'
The other took him at his word,
And followed as he led.
It was a spot which you may see
If ever you to Langdale go;
Into a chasm a mighty block
Hath fallen, and made a bridge of rock:
The gulf is deep below;
And, in a basin black and small,
Receives a lofty waterfall.

With staff in hand across the cleft
The challenger pursued his march;
And now, all eyes and feet, hath gained
The middle of the arch.
When list! he hears a piteous moan—
Again!—his heart within him dies—
His pulse is stopped, his breath is lost,
He totters, pallid as a ghost,
And, looking down, espies
A lamb, that in the pool is pent
Within that black and frightful rent.

The lamb had slipped into the stream,
And safe without a bruise or wound
The cataract had borne him down
Into the gulf profound.
His dam had seen him when he fell,
She saw him down the torrent borne;
And, while with all a mother's love
She from the lofty rocks above
Sent forth a cry forlorn,
The lamb, still swimming round and round,
Made answer to that plantive sound.

When he had learnt what thing it was,
That sent this rueful cry, I ween
The Boy recovered heart, and told
The sight which he had seen.
Both gladly now deferred their task;
Nor was there wanting other aid—
A Poet, one who loves the brooks,
Far better than the sages' books,
By chance had thither strayed;
And there the helpless lamb he found
By those huge rocks encompassed round.

He drew it from the troubled pool,
And brought it forth into the light:
The Shepherds met him with his charge,
An unexpected sight!
Into their arms the lamb they took,
Whose life and limbs the flood had spared;
Then up the steep ascent they hied,
And placed him at his mother's side;
And gently did the Bard
Those idle Shepherd-boys upbraid,
And bade them better mind their trade.

The Daffodils

I wander'd lonely as a cloud
That floats on high o'er vales and hills,
When all at once I saw a crowd,
A host of golden daffodils;
Beside the lake, beneath the trees
Fluttering and dancing in the breeze.

Continuous as the stars that shine
And twinkle on the milky way,
They stretch'd in never-ending line
Along the margin of a bay:
Ten thousand saw I at a glance,
Tossing their heads in sprightly dance.

The waves beside them danced; but they
Out-did the sparkling waves in glee:—
A poet could not but be gay
In such a jocund company:
I gazed—and gazed—but little thought
What wealth the show to me had brought.

For oft, when on my couch I lie
In vacant or in pensive mood,
They flash upon that inward eye

Which is the bliss of solitude;
And then my heart with pleasure fills,
And dances with the daffodils.

Airey-Force Valley

—*N*ot a breath of air
Ruffles the bosom of this leafy glen.
From the brook's margin, wide around, the trees
Are steadfast as the rocks; the brook itself,
Old as the hills that feed it from afar,
Doth rather deepen than disturb the calm
Where all things else are still and motionless.
And yet, even now, a little breeze, perchance
Escaped from boisterous winds that rage without,
Has entered, by the sturdy oaks unfelt,
But to its gentle touch how sensitive
Is the light ash! that, pendent from the brow
Of yon dim cave, in seeming silence makes
A soft eye-music of slow-waving boughs,
Powerful almost as vocal harmony
To stay the wanderer's steps and soothe his
    thoughts.

To the Cuckoo

O blithe new-comer! I have heard,
I hear thee and rejoice:
O Cuckoo! shall I call thee Bird,
Or but a wandering Voice?

While I am lying on the grass
Thy twofold shout I hear;
From hill to hill it seems to pass,
At once far off and near.

Though babbling only to the vale,
Of sunshine and of flowers,
Thou bringest unto me a tale
Of visionary hours.

Thrice welcome, darling of the Spring!
Even yet thou art to me
No bird, but an invisible thing,
A voice, a mystery;

The same whom in my school-boy days
I listen'd to; that Cry
Which made me look a thousand ways
In bush, and tree, and sky.

To seek thee did I often rove
Through woods and on the green;
And thou wert still a hope, a love;
Still long'd for, never seen!

And I can listen to thee yet;
Can lie upon the plain
And listen, till I do beget
That golden time again.

O blesséd Bird! the earth we pace
Again appears to be
An unsubstantial, faery place,
That is fit home for Thee!

FROM *Resolution and Independence*

*T*here was a roaring in the wind all night;
The rain came heavily and fell in floods;
But now the sun is rising calm and bright;
The birds are singing in the distant woods;
Over his own sweet voice the Stock-dove broods;
The Jay makes answer as the Magpie chatters;
And all the air is filled with pleasant noise of
    waters.

All things that love the sun are out of doors;
The sky rejoices in the morning's birth;
The grass is bright with rain-drops;—on the moors
The hare is running races in her mirth;
And with her feet she from the plashy earth
Raises a mist, that, glittering in the sun,
Runs with her all the way, wherever she doth run.

I was a Traveller then upon the moor,
I saw the hare that raced about with joy;
I heard the woods and distant waters roar;
Or heard them not, as happy as a boy;
The pleasant season did my heart employ:
My old remembrances went from me wholly;
And all the ways of men, so vain and melancholy.

Written in March

The Cock is crowing,
The stream is flowing,
The small birds twitter,
The lake doth glitter,
The green field sleeps in the sun;
The oldest and youngest
Are at work with the strongest;
The cattle are grazing,
Their heads never raising;
There are forty feeding like one!
Like an army defeated
The snow hath retreated,
And now doth fare ill
On the top of the bare hill;
The Ploughboy is whooping—anon—anon:
There's joy in the mountains;
There's life in the fountains;
Small clouds are sailing,
Blue sky prevailing;
The rain is over and gone!

BROTHERSWATER

Lines Written In Early Spring

I heard a thousand blended notes,
While in a grove I sate reclined,
In that sweet mood when pleasant thoughts
Bring sad thoughts to the mind.

To her fair works did Nature link
The human soul that through me ran;
And much it grieved my heart to think
What man has made of man.

Through primrose tufts, in that green bower,
The periwinkle trailed its wreaths;
And 'tis my faith that every flower
Enjoys the air it breathes.

The birds around me hopped and played,
Their thoughts I cannot measure:—
But the least motion which they made,
It seemed a thrill of pleasure.

The budding twigs spread out their fan,
To catch the breezy air;
And I must think, do all I can,
That there was pleasure there.

If this belief from heaven be sent,
If such be Nature's holy plan,
Have I not reason to lament
What man has made of man?

FROM *Margaret*

I roved o'er many a hill and many a dale,
With my accustomed load; in heat and cold,
Through many a wood and many an open ground,
In sunshine and in shade, in wet and fair,
Drooping or blithe of heart, as might befall;
My best companions now the driving winds,
And now the "trotting brooks" and whispering
    trees,
And now the music of my own sad steps,
With many a short-lived thought that passed
    between,
And disappeared.
        I journeyed back this way,
When, in the warmth of midsummer, the wheat
Was yellow; and the soft and bladed grass,
Springing afresh, had o'er the hay-field spread
Its tender verdure.

FROM *To M.H.*

*W*hen thou hadst quitted Esthwaite's
  pleasant shore,
And taken thy first leave of those green hills
And rocks that were the play-ground of thy youth,
Year followed year, my Brother! and we two,
Conversing not, knew little in what mould
Each other's mind was fashioned; and at length,
When once again we met in Grasmere Vale,
Between us there was little other bond
Than common feelings of fraternal love.
But thou, a School-boy, to the sea hadst carried
Undying recollections; Nature there
Was with thee; she, who loved us both, she still
Was with thee; and even so didst thou become
A *silent* Poet; from the solitude
Of the vast sea didst bring a watchful heart
Still couchant, an inevitable ear,
And an eye practised like a blind man's touch.
—Back to the joyless Ocean thou art gone;
Nor from this vestige of thy musing hours
Could I withhold thy honoured name,—and now
I love the fir-grove with a perfect love.
Thither do I withdraw when cloudless suns
Shine hot, or wind blows troublesome and strong;

And there I sit at evening, when the steep
Of Silver-how, and Grasmere's peaceful lake
And one green island, gleam between the stems
Of the dark firs, a visionary scene!
And while I gaze upon the spectacle
Of clouded splendour, on this dream-like sight
Of solemn loveliness, I think on thee,
My Brother, and on all which thou hast lost.
Nor seldom, if I rightly guess, while Thou,
Muttering the verses which I muttered first
Among the mountains, through the midnight watch
Art pacing thoughtfully the vessel's deck
In some far region, here, while o'er my head,
At every impulse of the moving breeze,
The fir-grove murmurs with a sea-like sound,
Alone I tread this path;—for aught I know,
Timing my steps to thine; and, with a store
Of undistinguishable sympathies,
Mingling most earnest wishes for the day
When we, and others whom we love, shall meet
A second time, in Grasmere's happy Vale.

FROM *To S. T. C. [Coleridge]*

*O*h! yet a few short years of useful life,
And all will be complete, thy race be run,
Thy monument of glory will be raised;
Then, though (too weak to tread the ways of truth)
This age fall back to old idolatry,
Though men return to servitude as fast
As the tide ebbs, to ignominy and shame
By nations sink together, we shall still
Find solace—knowing what we have learnt to know,
Rich in true happiness if allowed to be
Faithful alike in forwarding a day
Of firmer trust, joint labourers in the work
(Should Providence such grace to us vouchsafe)
Of their deliverance, surely yet to come.
Prophets of Nature, we to them will speak
A lasting inspiration, sanctified
By reason, blest by faith: what we have loved,
Others will love, and we will teach them how;
Instruct them how the mind of man becomes
A thousand times more beautiful than the earth
On which he dwells, above this frame of things
(Which, 'mid all revolution in the hopes
And fears of men, doth still remain unchanged)
In beauty exalted, as it is itself
Of quality and fabric more divine.

II

Samuel
Taylor Coleridge

Samuel Taylor Coleridge
(1772–1834)

*B*est remembered for his powerful imaginative poems "The Rime of the Ancient Mariner" and "Kubla Khan," Coleridge was a gifted poet and critic who fell short of achieving the promise of the *Lyrical Ballads*, copublished with Wordsworth in 1798. As friends and kindred spirits in the Lake District, they walked its hills and dales composing poetry in which Coleridge's vivid imagination was tempered by Wordsworth's deeper, slower response. Sadly, Coleridge and Wordsworth were estranged when the former suffered a long period of domestic turmoil and ill health, spending most of his time abroad. From 1806 Coleridge wrote little poetry, concentrating on his enduring works of literary criticism, notably *Biographia Literaria*, published in 1817.

Sonnet to The River Otter

*D*ear native Brook! wild
Streamlet of the West!
    How many various-fated years have past,
    What happy and what mournful hours, since last
I skimm'd the smooth thin stone along thy breast,
Numbering its light leaps! yet so deep imprest
Sink the sweet scenes of childhood, that mine eyes
    I never shut amid the sunny ray,
But straight with all their tints thy waters rise,
    Thy crossing plank, thy marge with willows grey,
And bedded sand that vein'd with various dyes
Gleam'd through thy bright transparence! On my
    way,
    Visions of Childhood! oft have ye beguil'd
Lone manhood's cares, yet waking fondest sighs:
    Ah! that once more I were a careless Child!

Youth and Age

*V*erse, a breeze 'mid blossoms straying,
Where Hope clung feeding, like a bee—
Both were mine! Life went a-maying
With Nature, Hope, and Poesy,
When I was young!
When I was young?—Ah, woful When!
Ah! for the change 'twixt Now and Then!
This breathing house not built with hands,
This body that does me grievous wrong,
O'er aery cliffs and glittering sands
How lightly then it flash'd along:
Like those trim skiffs, unknown of yore,
On winding lakes and rivers wide,
That ask no aid of sail or oar,
That fear no spite of wind or tide!
Nought cared this body for wind or weather
When Youth and I lived in't together.

Flowers are lovely; Love is flower-like;
Friendship is a sheltering tree;
O! the joys, that came down shower-like,
Of Friendship, Love, and Liberty,
Ere I was old!
Ere I was old? Ah woful Ere,

Which tells me, Youth's no longer here.
O Youth! for years so many and sweet,
'Tis known that Thou and I were one,
I'll think it but a fond conceit—
It cannot be, that Thou art gone!
Thy vesper-bell hath not yet toll'd:—

And thou wert aye a masker bold!
What strange disguise hast now put on
To make believe that Thou art gone!
I see these locks in silvery slips,
This drooping gait, this alter'd size:
But Springtide blossoms on thy lips,
And tears take sunshine from thine eyes!
Life is but Thought: so think I will
That Youth and I are housemates still.

Dew-drops are the gems of morning,
But the tears of mournful eve!
Where no hope is, life's a warning
—That only serves to make us grieve
With oft and tedious taking-leave,
Like some poor nigh-related guest
That may not rudely be dismist,
Yet hath out-stay'd his welcome while,
And tells the jest without the smile.

FROM *Dejection: An Ode*

I

*W*ell! If the Bard was weather-wise, who made
The grand old ballad of Sir Patrick Spence,
This night, so tranquil now, will not go hence
Unroused by winds, that ply a busier trade
Than those which mould yon cloud in lazy flakes,
Or the dull sobbing draft, that moans and rakes
Upon the strings of this Æolian lute,
Which better far were mute.
For lo! the New-moon winter-bright!
And overspread with phantom light,
(With swimming phantom light o'erspread
But rimmed and circled by a silver thread)
I see the old Moon in her lap, foretelling
The coming-on of rain and squally blast,
And oh! that even now the gust were swelling,
And the slant night-shower driving loud and fast!
Those sounds which oft have raised me, whilst they
    awed
And sent my soul abroad,
Might now perhaps their wonted impulse give,
Might startle this dull pain, and make it move
    and live!

II

A grief without a pang, void, dark, and drear,
A stifled, drowsy, unimpassioned grief,
Which finds no natural outlet, no relief,
In word, or sigh, or tear—
O Lady! in this wan and heartless mood,
To other thoughts by yonder throstle woo'd,
All this long eve, so balmy and serene,
Have I been gazing on the western sky,
And its peculiar tint of yellow green;
And still I gaze—and with how blank an eye!
And those thin clouds above, in flakes and bars,
That give away their motion to the stars:
Those stars, that glide behind them or between,
Now sparkling, now bedimmed, but always seen;
Yon crescent Moon, as fixed as if it grew
In its own cloudless, starless lake of blue;
I see them all so excellently fair,
I see, not feel, how beautiful they are!

FROM *Christabel*, PART II

*E*ach matin bell, the Baron saith,
Knells us back to a world of death,
These words Sir Leoline first said,
When he rose and found his lady dead:
These words Sir Leoline will say
Many a morn to his dying day!

And hence the custom and law began
That still at dawn the sacristan,
Who duly pulls the heavy bell
Five and forty beads must tell
Between each stroke—a warning knell,
Which not a soul can choose but hear
From Bratha Head to Wyndermere.

Saith Bracy the bard, So let it knell!
And let the drowsy sacristan
Still count as slowly as he can!
There is no lack of such, I ween,
As well fill up the space between.
In Langdale Pike and Witch's Lair,
And Dungeon-ghyll so foully rent,
With ropes of rock and bells of air
Three sinful sextons' ghosts are pent.
Who all give back, one after t'other,

The death note to their living brother;
And oft too, by the knell offended,
Just as their one! two! three! is ended,
The devil mocks the doleful tale
With a merry peal from Borrowdale.

A Thought Suggested By a View of Saddleback in Cumberland

On stern Blencartha's perilous height
The winds are tyrannous and strong;
And flashing forth unsteady light
From stern Blencartha's skiey height,
As loud the torrents throng!
Beneath the moon, in gentle weather,
They bind the earth and sky together.
But oh! the sky and all its forms, how quiet!
The things that seek the earth, how full of noise
and riot!

FROM *To William Wordsworth*

$\mathcal{E}$ve following eve,
Dear tranquil time, when the sweet sense of Home
Is sweetest! moments for their own sake hailed
And more desire, more precious, for thy song,
In silence listening, like a devout child,
My soul lay passive, by thy various strain
Driven as in surges now beneath the stars,
With momentary stars of my own birth,
Fair constellated foam, still darting off
Into the darkness; now a tranquil sea,
Outspread and bright, yet swelling to the moon.

And when—O Friend! my comforter and guide!
Strong in thyself, and powerful to give strength!—
Thy long sustained Song finally closed,
And thy deep voice had ceased—yet thou thyself
Wert still before my eyes, and round us both
That happy vision of belovéd faces—
Scarce conscious, and yet conscious of its close
I sate, my being blended in one thought
(Thought was it? or aspiration? or resolve?)
Absorbed, yet hanging still upon the sound—
And when I rose, I found my self in prayer.

FROM *A Stranger Minstrel*

*A*s late on Skiddaw's mount I lay supine,
Midway th' ascent, in that repose divine
When the soul centred in the heart's recess
Hath quaff'd its fill of Nature's loveliness,
Yet still beside the fountain's marge will stay

And fain would thirst again, again to quaff;
Then when the tear, slow travelling on its way,

Fills up the wrinkles of a silent laugh—
In that sweet mood of sad and humorous thought
A form within me rose, within me wrought
With such strong magic, that I cried aloud,
"Thou ancient Skiddaw by thy helm of cloud,
And by thy many-colour'd chasms deep,
And by their shadow that for ever sleep,
By yon small flaky mists that love to creep
Along the edges of those spots of light,
Those sunny islands on the smooth green height,

And by yon shepherds with their sheep,
And dogs and boys, a gladsome crowd,
That rush e'en now with clamour loud
Sudden from forth thy topmost cloud,
And by this laugh, and by this tear,
I would, old Skiddaw, she were here!"

FROM *An Ode to the Rain*

I have not once opened the lids of my eyes,
But I lie in the dark, as a blind man lies.
O Rain! that I lie listening to,
You're but a doleful sound at best:
I owe you little thanks, 'tis true,
For breaking thus my needful rest!
Yet if, as soon as it is light,
O Rain! you will but take your flight,
I'll neither rail, nor malice keep,
Though sick and sore for want of sleep.
But only now, for this one day,
Do go, dear Rain! do go away!

II

O Rain! with your dull two-fold sound,
The clash hard by, and the murmur all round!
You know, if you know aught, that we,
Both night and day, but ill agree:
For days and months, and almost years,
Have limped on through this vale of tears,
Since body of mine, and rainy weather,
Have lived on easy terms together.
Yet if, as soon as it is light,

O Rain! you will but take your flight,
Though you should come again to-morrow,
And bring with you both pain and sorrow;
Though stomach should sicken and knees should
    swell—
I'll nothing speak of you but well.
But only now for this one day,
Do go, dear Rain! do go away!

FROM *To The Nightingale*

Sister of love-lorn Poets, Philomel!
How many Bards in city garret pent,
While at their window they with downward eye
Mark the faint lamp-beam on the kennel'd mud,
And listen to the drowsy cry of Watchmen
(Those hoarse unfeather'd Nightingales of Time!),
How many wretched Bards address *thy* name,
And hers, the full-orb'd Queen that shines above.
But I *do* hear thee, and the high bough mark,
Within whose mild moon-mellow'd foliage hid
Thou warblest sad thy pity-pleading strains.

FROM *The Picture*

*T*hrough weeds and thorns, and matted underwood
I force my way; now climb, and now descend
O'er rocks, or bare or mossy, with wild foot
Crushing the purple whorts; while oft unseen,
Hurrying along the drifted forest-leaves,
The scared snake rustles. Onward still I toil,
I know not, ask not whither! A new joy,
Lovely as light, sudden as summer gust,
And gladsome as the first-born of the spring,
Beckons me on, or follows from behind,
Playmate, or guide! The master-passion quelled,
I feel that I am free. With dun-red bark
The fir-trees, and the unfrequent slender oak,
Forth from this tangle wild of bush and brake
Soar up, and form a melancholy vault
High o'er me, murmuring like a distant sea.
Here Wisdom might resort, and here Remorse;
Here too the love-lorn man, who, sick in soul.
And of this busy human heart aweary,
Worships the spirit of unconscious life
In tree or wild-flower.—Gentle lunatic!
If so he might not wholly cease to be,
He would far rather not be that he is;
But would be something that he knows not of,
In winds or waters, or among the rocks!

III

Robert Southey

Robert Southey
(1774–1843)

A native of Bristol, Southey was orphaned early in life and grew up in Bath with relatives. He had the rebellious temperament of the Romantic Age and was expelled from Westminster School for writing a satire on flogging. After two years at Oxford, he settled at Keswick in the Lake District and became close to Coleridge. Both admired the young Wordsworth and his commitment to a simpler, purer form of poetry. Most of Southey's long romantic poems are too florid for modern readers; they include *Thalaba, the Destroyer* (1801) and *The Curse of Kehama* (1810). Many prefer his prose works, including the *Life of Nelson* (1813), the multi-volume *History of the Peninsular War* (1823–32), and—surprisingly—"The Story of Goldilocks and the Three Bears." Southey was named poet laureate in 1813.

FROM *Rhymes for the Nursery*

*F*rom its sources which well
In the Tarn on the fell;
From its fountains
In the mountains,
Its rills and its gills;
Through moss and through brake,
It runs and it creeps
For a while, till it sleeps
In its own little Lake.
And thence at departing,
Awakening and starting,
It runs through the reeds
And away it proceeds,
Through meadow and glade,
In sun and in shade,
And through the wood-shelter,
Among crags in its flurry,
Helter-skelter,
Hurry-scurry.
Here it comes sparkling,
And there it comes darkling—
Now smoking and frothing
Its tumult and wrath in,
Till in this rapid race

On which it is bent,
It reaches the place
Of its steep descent.

* * *

The Cataract strong
Then plunges along,
Striking and raging
As if a war waging
Its caverns and rocks among:
Rising and leaping,
Sinking and creeping,
Swelling and sweeping,
Showering and springing,
Flying and flinging,
Writhing and ringing,
Eddying and whisking,
Spouting and frisking,
Turning and twisting,
Around and around
With endless rebound!
Smiting and fighting,
A sight to delight in;
Confounding, astounding,
Dizzying and deafening the ear with its sound.

* * *

Retreating and beating and meeting and sheeting,
Delaying and straying and playing and spraying,
Advancing and prancing and glancing and
    dancing,
Recoiling, turmoiling and toiling and boiling,
And gleaming and streaming and steaming and
    beaming,
And rushing and flushing and brushing and
    gushing,
And flapping and rapping and clapping and
    slapping,
And curling and whirling and purling and twirling,
And thumping and plumping and bumping and
    jumping,
And dashing and flashing and splashing and
    clashing;
And so never ending, but always descending,
Sounds and motions for ever and ever are
    blending,
All at once and all o'er, with a mighty uproar,
And this way the Water comes down at Lodore.

LODORE FALLS, DERWENTWATER

FROM *A Vision of Judgement*

'*T*was at that sober hour when the light of day is
    receding,
And from surrounding things the hues wherewith
    day has adorn'd them
Fade, like the hopes of youth, till the beauty of earth
    is departed:
Pensive, though not in thought, I stood at the
    window, beholding
Mountain and lake and vale; the valley disrobed of
    its verdure;
Derwent retaining yet from eve a glassy reflection
Where his expanded breast, then still and smooth as
    a mirror,
Under the woods reposed; the hills that, calm and
    majestic,
Lifted their heads in the silent sky, from far
    Glaramara
Bleacrag, and Maidenmawr, to Grizdal and
    westermost Withop.
Dark and distinct they rose. The clouds hath
    gather'd above them
High in the middle air, huge, purple, pillowy masses,
While in the west beyond was the last pale tint of the
    twilight:

Green as a stream in the glen whose pure and
    chrysolite waters
Flow o'er a schistous bed, and serene as the age of the
    righteous.
Earth was hush'd and still; all motion and sound
    were suspended:
Neither man was heard, bird, beast, nor humming of
    insect,
Only the voice of the Greta, heard only when all is in
    stillness.
Pensive I stood and alone, the hour and the scene
    had subdued me,
And as I gazed in the west, where Infinity seem'd to
    be open,
Yearn'd to be free from time, and felt that this life is a
    thraldom.

FROM *Letters from England*

*T*he pride of the Lake of Keswick is the head, where
the mountains of Borrowdale bound the prospect, in
a wilder and grander manner than words can ade-
quately describe. The cataract of Lodore thunders down
its eastern side through a chasm in the rocks, which
are wooded with birch and ash trees. It is a little river,

flowing from a small lake upon the mountain about a league distant. The water, though there had been heavy rains, was not adequate to the channel;—indeed it would require a river of considerable magnitude to fill it,—yet it is at once the finest work and instrument of rock and water that I have ever seen or heard.

LODORE FALLS, DERWENTWATER

On Bala Hill

With many a weary step at length I gain
Thy summit, and the cool breeze plays
Cheerily round my brow—as hence the gaze
Returns to dwell upon the journey'd plain.

'Twas a long way and tedious!—to the eye
Tho' fair th' extended Vale, and fair to view
The falling leaves of many a faded hue
That eddy in the wild gust moaning by!

Ev'n so it far'd with Life! in discontent
Restless thro' Fortune's mingled scenes I went,
Yet wept to think they would return no more!
O' cease fond heart! in such sad thoughts to roam,
For surely thou ere long shalt reach thy home,
And pleasant is the way that lies before.

IV

Thomas De Quincey

Thomas De Quincey
(1785–1859)

A renowned essayist, De Quincey is best known for his autobiographical *Confessions of an English Opium Eater*, first published in 1821. A native of Manchester, he had an unhappy boyhood and began taking opium while a student at Oxford to relieve the pain of neuralgia. His dependence on the drug was lifelong. In 1809 he settled in the Lake District and became friendly with Wordsworth and Coleridge. His reminiscences of the Lake Poets form an important chapter in the history of English Romanticism. After leaving the Lake District in 1820, he moved to London and then to Edinburgh, where he wrote for *Blackwood's* magazine. In 1856 he published a revised and expanded version of the *Confessions*.

Airey Force

FROM *RECOLLECTIONS OF THE LAKE POETS*

*T*here is, on the western side of Ulleswater, a fine cataract (or, in the language of the country, a *force*) known by the name of Airey Force; and it is of importance enough, especially in rainy seasons, to attract numerous visitors from among 'the Lakers'. Thither, with some purpose of sketching, not the whole scene, but some picturesque features of it, Miss Smith had gone, quite unaccompanied. The road to it lies through Gobarrow Park; and it was usual, at that time, to take a guide from the family of the Duke of Norfolk's keeper, who lived in Lyulph's Tower—a solitary hunting lodge, built by his Grace for the purpose of an annual visit which he used to pay to his estates in that part of England. She, however,… had declined to encumber her motions with such an attendant; consequently she was alone. For half an hour or more, she continued to ascend, and, being a good 'cragswoman', she had reached an altitude much beyond what would generally be thought corresponding to the time. The path had vanished altogether; but she continued to pick out one for herself among the stones, sometimes receding from the *force*, sometimes approaching it, according to the openings allowed by the scattered masses of rock.

The Vale of Grasmere
FROM *RECOLLECTIONS OF THE LAKE POETS*

*S*o far from neglecting Wordsworth, it is a fact that twice I had undertaken a long journey expressly for the purpose of paying my respects to Wordsworth; twice I came so far as the little rustic inn (then the sole inn of the neighbourhood) at Church Coniston; and on neither occasion could I summon confidence enough to present myself before him…

Twice, as I have said, did I advance as far as the Lake of Coniston; which is about eight miles from the church of Grasmere, and once I absolutely went forwards from Coniston to the very gorge of Hammerscar, from which the whole Vale of Grasmere suddenly breaks upon the view in a style of almost theatrical surprise, with its lovely valley stretching before the eye in the distance, the lake lying immediately below, with its solemn ark-like island of four and a half acres in size seemingly floating on its surface, and its exquisite outline on the opposite shore, revealing all its little bays and wide sylvan margin, feathered to the edge with wild flowers and ferns. In one quarter, a little wood, stretching for about half a mile towards the outlet of the lake; more directly in opposition to the spectator, a few green fields; and beyond them, just two bowshots from the water, a little white cottage gleaming from the midst of trees, with a vast and seemingly never-ending series of ascents rising above it to the height of more than three thousand feet. That little cottage was Wordsworth's from the time of his marriage, and earlier; in fact, from the beginning of the century to the year 1808. Afterwards, for many a year, it was mine. Catching one hasty glimpse of this loveliest of landscapes, I retreated like a guilty thing, for I feared I might be surprised by Wordsworth, and then returned faintheartedly to Coniston, and so to Oxford, *re infectâ.*

FROM A LETTER TO WILLIAM WORDSWORTH

*B*ut may I say in general, without the smallest exaggeration, that the whole aggregate of pleasure I have received from some eight or nine other poets that I have been able to find since the world began—falls infinitely short of what those two enchanting volumes have singly afforded me;—that your name is with me forever linked to the lovely scenes of nature;—and that not yourself only but that each place and object you have mentioned—and all the souls in that delightful community of your's—to me 'Are dearer than the sun.' With such opinions, it is not surprising that I should so earnestly and humbly sue for your friendship;—it is not surprising that the hope of that friendship should have sustained me through two years of a life passed partially in the world—and therefore not passed in happiness;—that I should have breathed forth my morning and my evening orisons for the accomplishment of that hope;—that I should now consider it as the only object worthy of my nature or capable of rewarding my pains. Sometimes indeed, in the sad and dreary vacuity of worldly intercourse, this hope will touch those chords that have power to rouse me from the lethargy of despair; and sometimes, from many painful circumstances—many bitter recollections, it is my only refuge.

At Kirkstone Pass with the Wordsworths

FROM *RECOLLECTIONS OF THE LAKE POETS*

*F*rom Ambleside—and without one foot of intervening flat ground—begins to rise the famous ascent of Kirkstone; after which, for three long miles, all riding in a cart drawn by one horse becomes impossible. The ascent is computed at three miles, but is, probably, a little more. In some parts it is almost frightfully steep; for the road, being only the original mountain track of shepherds, gradually widened and improved from age to age (especially since the era of tourists began), is carried over ground which no engineer, even in alpine countries, would have viewed as practicable. In ascending, this is felt chiefly as an obstruction and not as a peril, unless where there is a risk of the horses backing; but in the reverse order, some of these precipitous descents are terrific; and yet once, in utter darkness, after midnight, and the darkness irradiated only by continual streams of lightning, I was driven down this whole descent, at a full gallop, by a young woman—the carriage being a light one, the horses frightened, and the descents at some critical parts of the road, so literally like the sides of a house, that it was difficult to keep the fore wheels from pressing upon the hind legs of the horses…The innkeeper of Ambleside, or Lowwood, will not mount this formidable hill without four horses. The leaders you are not required to take beyond the first three miles; but, of course, they are glad if you will take them on the whole stage of nine miles, to Patterdale; and, in that case, there is a real luxury at hand for those who enjoy velocity of motion. The descent into Patterdale is much above two miles; but such is the propensity for flying down hills in Westmoreland, that I have found the descent accomplished in about six minutes, which is at the rate of eighteen miles an hour; the various turnings of the road making the speed much more sensible to the traveller.